Knowing Me, Knowing You

Kristina McGee-Kompel

Presentation by *BookLeaf Publishing*

Web: www.bookleafpub.com

E-mail: info@bookleafpub.com

ISBN: 9789357441414

First edition 2023

ACKNOWLEDGEMENT

Thank you to everyone who has supported me throughout my writing process! I would especially like to thank my parents and grandparents who always told me I could do whatever I put my mind to. My friends for being some of my first readers and editors. And finally to my husband for always encouraging me to step out of my comfort zone and try even when things get tough.

Hickory Brown

I sit silently staring piercingly at porous brick
walls.
Dark black coffee glistens, and bitter steam
grazes my nose.
The grit between my teeth grinds
bitter
burnt
slightly sweet.
Remnants and reminders of warm and bitter
coffee,
needing a splash of cream.

The Magic of Sight

oculus uterque
cones and rods and colors
watching
witnessing
darting back and forth
zip zap
electric signals fire
the image formed
upside down
curved by the eye
flipped by the brain
cerebrum
13 milliseconds later
I see you

Concrete Noun

love
/ləv/

A personified feeling in Roman history.

an intense feeling of deep affection
noun

intense interest or pleasure in something
noun

It is never really concrete but fluid.

Teakettle

She was a quiet one...

Usually pondering thoughts and ideas
she didn't move much
she sat there
on the shiny surface
her peaceful ways often tested.

Sometimes she was filled
with unbearable emotions
a fire was lit beneath her
an irritable heat
one that didn't just disappear.

Liquid slowly dripped down her sides
pressure built up
higher and higher
until she began to shake
steam seeping from her mouth
and finally
she screamed.

Cakewalk

when i was a child i learned to walk one step at a
time
one
two
i had the support of my family and the people
around me
      one
          two
i learned to walk with my own two feet in the
end
      one
          two
the first time my heart was broken I thought I
would never love again
dramatic
i know
then i met you and learned to love and walk
again with your support
ultimately it was me opening up to myself that
allowed me to put my
first foot forward
then the second.

Dreams

Where do we go when we fall asleep?
Collecting leaves in our minds into piles.
Lost in our thoughts and memories.
Sitting behind the glass that is our eyes.
What will I dream about tonight?
I close my eyes and let my brain take the reigns.
Jumping into that pile of leaves.

The Dragon's Glow

Before the tall window stood a girl
a brush pressed against her lips.
She sighed while staring at the simplistic art
that lay in front of her eyes,
the dragon's scales dull without the rainbow
of light that would soon add beauty to the page.

Droplets of cool white color touched the page
before a gentle blue hue became the sky, a girl's
imagination. An imagination flowing ideas like a
rainbow
flowed into a simmering pot of gold. Teeth bit
into red lips,
red from a constant worry that the eyes will see.
The eyes
of others will look at the art

with shame and disappointment, that this art
would be placed on a wall for the world to see.
Beauty
is shown in her twinkling eyes.
She was just a teenage girl,
with a love of a lizard-like beast. Her lips
turned up and quickly a rainbow

of color danced across the page. Rainbows
of ruby reds, piercing purples and other colors
became the art
and talent of her brush. Upturned in a content
grin, lips
shined with the dragon's reflection. Pure beauty
gave joy as this young creature, this young girl,
 saw her piece take form and she looked into his
eyes,

the dragon's amazing eyes, large yellow globes,
these eyes
were daunting and terrifying compared to the
rainbow
of scales and traces of brighter oils the girl
strategically placed on the blank canvas.
Slowing forming art
a once simplistic piece of stretched cloth now
displayed beauty
as well as a horror of sharp fangs and yellow
orbs. The lips

turned downwards towards the earth and
quivered. She bit her lips
once more and soft drops of glass escaped her
eyes.
They fell quickly as she realized the beauty
she created had been finished far too soon. The
rainbow

of scales taunted her, trying to make her start
over, the art
 was complete though. And she was no longer a
girl.

She is an artist with rainbow-like eyes,
a paintbrush touching her soft lips.
A spectacular girl who made a rainbow touch
the page.

Home

Home is fluid
moving to and fro
it's where you are
with those who bring
sparkles to your eyes
and make your heart beat.

Home is camaraderie
trust and memories
of laughter and tears
frustration and fears
friendship isn't easy
but I'm home with you.

Home is generations
grandparents whose smiles
wrinkle with wisdom
parents and siblings
enemies when wild and younger
daily texts to remind you care.

Home is love
where I am in your arms
safe and secure.

I am home with you.

Falling for You

Love is a symbiotic parasitic creature.
Worming its way into your heart.
Additive and resistant to any drug.
It burrows deep
      setting
          down
             roots.

I Felt It From the First Embrace

I shared it with you
I felt today
tomorrow
forever
it's love.

I felt it from the first embrace
a touch
a dance
all I know is the feeling.

I felt it from the first embrace
my heart beating
ba-dump
ba-dump
ba-dump
what I know now
I really knew then
I felt it from the first embrace.

Red Roses

Love is like a red red rose...
A cliche of petals.

Love should be yellow roses.
Joyous appreciation.
Symbolic of friendship.
My love for you is warm and cheerful.
Cheerful and Warm.

Love is anything but a red red rose.

Grow Tall

Stumbling onto the street frustrated by the
doorframe that trips
Items sprawling all over the sidewalk
Phone cracking as its corner smacks the mixture
of rocks
Coins rolling from the wallet's interior
Mug crashing into a minimum of twenty pieces
Bitter coffee crying into the gaps and touching
soil barely there
Feeding the weeds and giving them a chance to
grow.

Breathing

Breathing is supposed to be automatic.

Your brain remembers how to make your lungs
expand
oxygen moving to your blood
carbon dioxide making its way out
exhaled through your breath
then I met you
breathed in and froze.

I had to learn to breathe again.

Under the Big Sky

I'm mountains of royalty standing tall with pride
and fertile valleys filled with blood-red fruits.
I'm sunrises that bleed gold onto the ground
and sunsets that burn gentle pinks and violent
oranges into the sky.
I'm tall Ponderosa Pines, plum Bitterroots,
and the gentle swaying of Bluebunch
Wheatgrass.
I'm raging rivers, cascading streams,
and every natural hot spring.
I'm a curious grizzly, a song of the meadowlark,
and the minuscule fry of a Cutthroat.
I'm deathly cold winters that wrack the body
with shivers
and scorching summers that set the hills ablaze.
I'm from the wings of a blessed Mourning Cloak
Butterfly
and the bones of a duck-like dinosaur,
I'm the blue glass Sapphire
and the swirling grays and whites of an Agate.
I'm Oro y Plata,
the winter of 1889.
Within myself, Montana resides.

Find Yourself

Filling a cup with passion.
You can't pour from an empty bucket.
Find yourself.
Help yourself first.
Fill your cup.

The Cat

A fun little being that is perpetually annoyed
by the existence of everything.
His attitude drips with the raw emotion of
disapproval
that is necessary for his existence.

My heart
swells when I hold him and feel his bee-like
buzzing.
He forces strong vibrations
of love to strike my heart.

Gratitude

Now I know what responsibility means
      But I won't admit I was wrong
I remember your lectures
      Being told about pride
I remember saying I know
      I didn't know
I remember being overconfident
      and you teaching me
        time and time again
Thank you
You were right

Dreams

Calm break of the day
For a romantic, love soars
into the horizon.

Grandma's House

21

Relaxing summers
An enclosed patio, sits
with chicken noodle soup.

A Dream

My honeymoon, you inspire me to write.
How I love the way you look, walk and soar,
Invading my mind day and through the night,
Always dreaming of you.

Wild sun heats the Oregon beaches in June,
How do I love you? Let me count the ways.
I love your brains, kindness, and humour.
Thinking of you fills my days.

Remember my words when we're apart.
My love for you is all comsuming.

Grandpa's Garden

Early summertime
A lovely garden grows
Tilling rows of beans.

www.ingramcontent.com/pod-product-compliance
Lightning Source LLC
LaVergne TN
LVHW050301200726
843509LV00015B/3100